MEMORIES OF
BOGNOR REGIS & CHICHESTER

To my husband Ken,
who must wonder "What Next?"

And to all those whose memories are stirred
by mention of time or place.

Memories of
Bognor Regis
& Chichester
in the 1930s, 40s, 50s & 60s

Sylvia Olliver

Woodfield

First edition, published in 2003 by

WOODFIELD PUBLISHING
Bognor Regis, West Sussex PO21 5EL
United Kingdom
www.woodfieldpublishing.com

ISBN 1-903953-49-9

CONTENTS

Bognor Regis from the air c 1930.

INTRODUCTION

When Bognorians and long-term residents meet up they invariably talk of times past – the Pavilion, the Pier, the Esplanade Theatre etc, so I felt that nostalgia is not always a subject of the past!

Other books about Bognor Regis have included local history information so I decided to write down some of my memories and to include Chichester as it also holds many memories of happy times.

Memories of my wartime childhood in Yorkshire have also been included. So many children's lives were turned upside down during that period. On reflection, I believe that it prepared me for any turmoil I might meet in later life. I also received a valuable piece of advice when the headmaster told me to 'stand up and fight back'.

Postcards from the times mentioned have also been included to illustrate my memories.

Sylvia Olliver
Bognor Regis, 2003

Hotham Park c1950.

West Promenade and Sands, Bognor Regis   8023

The promenade in the early 1960s.

ABOUT THE AUTHOR

Sylvia Olliver has been married to Ken for 35 years. She has a son, John, from her previous marriage, a stepson, Stephen and a grandson, Ryan.

Ken was also born and bred in Bognor Regis (Hawthorn Road) one of eight children; he is now the only survivor. He can remember when Hawthorn Road was so traffic-free that he could whip a top along the road!

Sylvia loves her home town and has served on the town council for 13 years. She is proud to have served the town as Mayor three times and Deputy Mayor three times (she is Deputy Mayor at the present time).

Sylvia has also served as a West Sussex County councillor for ten years and an Arun District Councillor for 13 years (she is currently an Arun District Councillor). She has also been a Bersted Parish Councillor for 18 years (and is still serving in that capacity).

The threat to demolish Bognor Town Hall 18 years ago was the reason for Sylvia to seek election in the first place.

Sylvia finds solace in writing poems and has had a number of them published.

KIDDIES' CORNER, HOTHAM PARK
BOGNOR REGIS
444.

Young at heart

Look beyond the eyes a little dimmed by age,
Look beyond the wrinkles, for there is a page
in life's book with each and every line,
Some deep-etched, some very fine.

For life brings its stories to unfold
Some mundane, some not to be told,
But remember that what you now see
Is an older version of the real me.

For always there has been a part
Where I remember and am young at heart.
I remember my parents, so loving and true,
I remember softly saying "I do."

The cradling of my baby son
The first time he echoed "Mum!"
My grandson saying "I love you Nan!"
Yes, life's pages sometimes hold a lovely plan.

For it's in our hands to make it so,
To bring joy so that love will grow,
To smile even when we feel down,
Laughter lines instead of a frown.

For to be young at heart,
Means that we can still play a part
In this wonderful world where we live
For we still have so much to give.

Sylvia Olliver 2003

When I was a child...

When I was born in 1930 if a pregnant woman was thought to be having a difficult time at childbirth it was wise to return to her parents home for the birth, and that was how I came to be born in my Grandparents home at 204 Orchard Street, Chichester, 7 miles away from my parents home at 1 Sudley Terrace in Bognor Regis High Street.

My father had to cycle back and forth to work until I was two weeks old and returned to our family home, he was a milk man at that time and had to be at work at 4.30 a.m. do two rounds and then wash his own milk bottles. Later when he worked for another dairy a horse was used to pull the milk cart, he also had to clean the horse down daily as well. The horse's name was 'Snowy' as his name suggested he was white. I loved to help my father on a Saturday round, sitting behind the horse was quite an experience at times!!

Although my mother was only 21 years old when I was born I was to be their only child. At times I was very lonely so grew to look forward to the weekly bus ride to my Grandparents home. The trips started when we lived in Kenilworth Road.

We used to get up even earlier on that day when my Mother always polished the linoleum downstairs on her hands and knees using Mansion polish. The linoleum was red with green and blue patterns similar to the Indian carpets. Rugs were placed strategically around and it was a well known fact with people who called that "you could see your face in Flo's floor" and so it was a rather dangerous venture to tread on one of the rugs which would slide from under you. We had six Broadbent chairs which Mum would let me help by dusting their legs. I still have one of those chairs.

My Grandparents had nine children - six girls and three boys - of which my mother was fourth. Three of those were born after the First World War so I had two Aunts and an Uncle ranging five to eleven years older than me. The comings and goings of Auntie Audrey and Vera and Uncle Ron's friends to Grandma's gave me a strong sense of "family", also most of my cousins living around that area calling in was very enjoyable - Grandma was a real "Featherbed Grandma", soft to the touch, kindly and loving.

Grandma often looked after me when Mum and Dad worked an evening at a Police Ball. Mum would put me on the bus knowing that I would be met at the bus stop outside Chichester Cathedral, I can still remember sitting on the long seat just inside the bus so that the Conductor could keep an eye on me and the benign smiles I would receive from the passengers.

My Mother did letting in the summer, so I was very lucky as visitors with children would also take me on the beach with them to keep their child or children company. I particularly liked it if they hired a beach hut for their stay as we stayed on the beach all day. Bright pictures painted on tin buckets, the nose twitching smell of the handles rusty at the joins, wooden spades, using a thumb to push up the Snofrute ice through its triangular cardboard wrapping, Punch and Judy, donkeys plodding back and forth across the sand, at the end of the day the tangy sea smell of my body - all happy memories. I have photographs showing me walking along clutching bucket and spade in the company of people and children whose names I do not now know.

A number of the visitors used to return every year and became family friends, one of the little girls proudly told me her birthday was 9th September 1930 and as that was also mine we became friends, but unfortunately lost touch, I often wonder about her on "our birthday". The war started when I was six days off my ninth birthday, it stopped all the sea side holidays and split everything asunder - but that's another story!!

My father was very fond of the countryside and some Sunday afternoons we would walk around the lovely Sussex lanes or hire bikes for Mum and I so that we could travel further afield. The pink and white milk-maids, the vetch and the smell of cowslips was such a simple pleasure. Sometimes we would catch the "Silver Queen" charabanc - as it's name suggests it was painted silver - in Bognor Regis and we would then travel to Slindon Woods to pick Bluebells, it was a local joke to say that courting couples went there bluebelling but always returned without any!

I used to "help" my father in the garden, he used to wonder why all the lupin plants popped up all over the borders until he found me opening the pods and pressing the seeds into the earth, they were so tall and graceful and smelt peppery. He also liked to grow dark mauve, blue and brown velvety Iris'.

When I was about three years old I remember picking my Mother a bunch of bright red flowers (which popped), I had to stand on my toes to reach them. When Dad came home she showed them to him and I wondered why they smiled. Years later I found out that they were runner bean flowers!!

Dad played football for one of the local teams. I was brought up to attend football matches, thoroughly enjoying the away matches when the charabanc would stop on the way home when the children would have lemonade and crisps and something stronger for the adults, always a good hearted time without any trouble.

Dad had spent nine years as a Bandsman in The Somerset Light Infantry before coming to Bognor in 1928, so the Bands playing in the Bandstands on Bognor's promenade were always a draw for my Dad and as he played the bass in the British Legion Band he was always playing at Fetes and Carnivals, also Carols at Christmas time under the gas lamps around Bognor Regis. I tried to play his bass but try as I might I couldn't get a sound out of it. The bass was kept under my bed so I knew that there wouldn't be room for anyone to hide, but still peeped under there every night when I said my prayers.

My Mother belonged to the British Legion Women's section, once a week she would attend their meetings or social events. In the school holidays I would accompany her to Tea Dances where she taught me the Valetta, St. Bernard's Waltz, Old Fashioned Waltz and other dances of that era, but my favourite dance was the Palais Glide where we would link up in lines and sing "Horsey, Horsey Don't You Stop". My hair smelt scorched as my Mother crimped it with curling irons which she heated in the fire or gas burner - Californian Poppy and Evening in Paris was the lovely scent wafting from the ladies. Powder puffs nestled in georgette handkerchiefs, dainty pencils with a tassle hanging were all part of that decade. When I see those items for sale at Antique Fairs I am immediately transported back in time to that gentle time of my childhood.

I was a very lucky child to have a happy family home by the sea and a "Featherbed Grandma" in a beautiful Cathedral City - Chichester just seven miles away.

Indeed a time of 'Kolynos' toothpaste, 'Camp' coffee, 'Lincoln Cream' and 'Nice' biscuits - a time to remember with love and thanks to hard working, loving and loyal parents who both died aged sixty two.

Gt Uncle George, Sylvia, Gt Aunty Daisy & Mum, coach park, Gloucester Road, Bognor, waiting for the coach to take George & Daisy home to Newbury Park Ilford

1931 outside Storey & Son, butchers, fruiterers and grocers at 1 Sudley Terrace, High St, Bognor. Sylvia Knight (later Olliver) with William Pengelly(Sylvia and parents lived above the shop).

c1933 on Bognor Beach, Sylvia (centre) with two friends.

Sylvia & Mother (Florence Knight), Bognor beach 1932.

c1932, Sylvia in bonnet aged about 2 years in the High Street opposite Staleys and the Sussex Hotel.

Dad, Fred Knight (on right) and friend on Bognor beach, 1930.

c1937 Sylvia with Bill and Win Pengelly and little Albert Pengelly from Plymouth.

Sylvia (standing) and friend on Bognor beach c1937.

Sylvia (in water) with friend, WestEnd, Bognor 1937.

My Father, Frederick John Knight (4.2.1905-6.7.1967 when a Somerset Light Infantry bandsman. Taken in 1928 in Worthing before leaving the Army after 9 years' service, having joined when he was 14.

Uncle Bill Pengelly dipping my feet, 1930 or 31.

Dick Clemens (centre) outside Bedford (now Unicorn) Hotel. Dick's letter to my father in 1928 resulted in his coming to Bognor.

PUTTING GREEN
BOGNOR.

This postcard is the reason I am here… It was written to my father just before he left the Somerset Light Infantry in 1928 by his friend Dick Clemens, who had served with him in the army and was now working at the Bedford hotel in Bognor Regis. Dick tells him of the likelihood of a job at the hotel. Percy Goodwin the landlord was also chairman of the Bognor Regis football team and knew that my father had played for his regiment, so was interested in him on both counts.

It is also strange that the Corner House Restaurant is depicted, because it is where my mother worked. One day she cut her finger and went into the "jug and bottle" bar at the Bedford hotel to get a quick "pick me up" and there met my father. They married in November 1929; one year and four months after my father received this postcard.

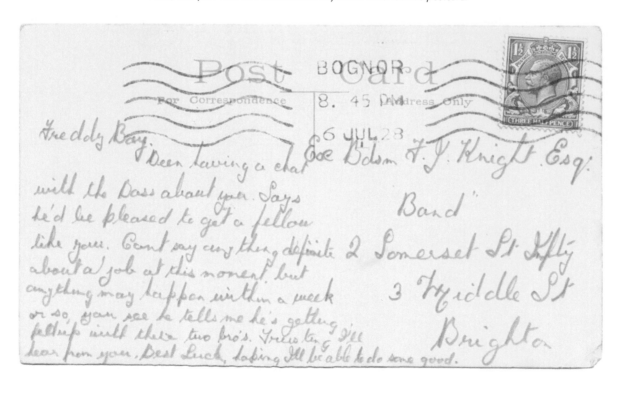

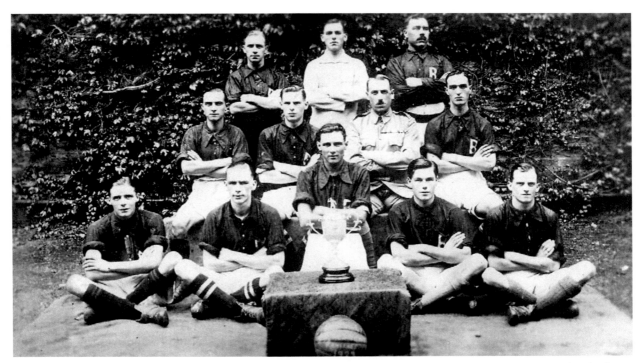

Winners of the inter-detachment football tournament held at Ranikhet, India, August 1923. Somerset Light Infantry beat the Cheshire Regiment 3-2. Fred Knight (my father) is in the middle row, second left. His friend Dick Clemens is in the front row, second left. In the middle row, second from right, is A.H Cook, who was to become chief warder at the Tower of London and also to receive the DCM, MM and BEM. He was known to us as 'Cooksey' and he was a friend of my paternal grandfather. When we visited the Tower of London he acted as our personal escort and consequently we saw parts of the building that are not normally on show to the public.

A.H. Cook (Cooksey) DCM, MM, BEM (seated centre) in uniform as Chief Warder at the Tower of London.

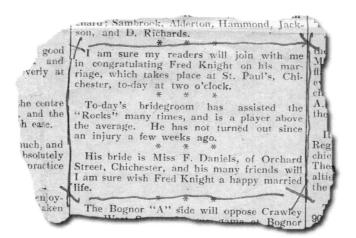

An excerpt from the Bognor Post, November 16th 1929

Bognor United 1931/32

Back row, left to right: Jerry Ursell, Reg Bailey, Albie Blackmore, Tom West, ('Dreamy' Sharp?), Fred Knight, Frank Jutton, Charlie Powell.
Front row, left to right: Jack Butcher, Jackie Ide, Jack Schooley, Jack Hammond, Sid Hammond.

*The Silver Queen bus ran a service between Bognor and Slindon; seen here on Bognor promenade.
We used to catch this bus to visit the bluebell woods.*

*Bognor Regis British Legion brass band in the 1930s. Fred Knight (my father) is in the back row third from right. Percy Woolard, the
bandmaster is in the front row (with baton).*

On the move

We moved to a house named 'Junette' in Chichester Road; it is still there although vastly altered into flats. The Royal Parade of shops had just been built so it must have been 1932 or 1933. the estate around them was in the process of being built. My parents walked me around this vast area of builder's materials and newly-started houses, it was a hive of activity. It must have appeared like Eldorado to them. The houses cost just £600, but in those days men were only paid £2/10 shillings per week, so even at that price they were well beyond their means.

One of my mother's friends moved into one of the new bungalows and I was fascinated to see that the kitchen table and seating, also the ironing board, unfolded from the walls and then neatly folded back into cupboards.

Whilst we lived there my parents would walk around to the 'Stamp House' pub, also named the 'Rising Sun'. One of the rooms had pictures made out of stamps all around the walls with festoons made from stamps hanging down. We would sit in the back garden in the evening and I can remember the bats flying around.

The new houses being beyond their means, my parents then moved to Kenilworth Road, three houses away from the twitten which led to Hawthorn Road at the junction of Nyewood Lane, a straight walk to the sea and a further step nearer to mum's dream of a house in town where she could have the summer visitors to supplement dad's wages.

Our landlord and landlady were Billy and Eve White, who had a small dance band. They played in the hall at the end of the pier. Eve used to play the piano for the silent films. During the war they joined ENSA and played to the troops all over the world. They became our friends and were a delightful and caring couple.

I started school when we were living at Kenilworth Road and it was a lovely walk to Nyewood Church of England School, then situated in Richmond Avenue. Hawthorn hedging grew along the corner of Hawthorn Road and up Nyewood Lane, the bright pink and white flowers had such a wonderful perfume. One day I gingerly picked a small bunch for my mother on my way home from school, but she would not take them into the house as she was superstitious about them. She would not have catkins from the tree (or lilac either) in the house.

Wild dog daisies grew in the field where the first Kyoto Court flats were built. Two beautiful horse chestnut trees grew out onto the edge of the road where it curved.

On Saints days we were marched from school along Wood Street through a path at the end where it meets Charlwood Street, through the grounds and then into St Wilfred's Church. On my first visit I dropped my collection money of one penny onto the floor and was severely reprimanded by Miss Steed. From then on I was terrified about repeating the offence.

In class Miss Steed was very strict, making us sit straight-backed with our arms folded behind our backs. Our reading books were printed in orange, black and white and the pictures were only in those colours (one of many memories of school). The headmaster was Mr Redford ('Fuzzy' was his nickname). Later on he was ordained and became the Reverend Redford.

We gathered in the playground on Empire day when the flag was raised; we sang 'Jerusalem' and other hymns.

I was very disappointed not to be selected for the nativity play. We were all asked to sing and it was noted that I did not sing in tune so I was the only child not on stage when all the parents turned up. I can still remember sitting with my parents watching the play.

Electricity was installed in our house in Kenilworth Road; what an upheaval that caused!

In those days there were no cars down our road. I swapped my Edwardian doll's pram with a little girl from Mayfield Road for her little bicycle which I could ride up Mayfield Road into Pevensey Road and back home without encountering a single car.

One of the houses had a hedge which was inhabited by pretty little pearl-backed snails which I loved to collect to watch them and would return them at the end of the day. Unfortunately one day I forgot to return them and they crawled out of my coat pocket overnight, leaving silver trails over ours and our visitors coats on the hall stand. My mother did not share my interest in snails!

Once a week my mother would meet me from school in Richmond Avenue and we would walk along Aldwick Road into Canada Grove to the Co-op where mother did some shopping. Then we would walk back home to Kenilworth Road down Linden Road back onto Hawthorn Road. Quite a round-trip for my little legs, but we didn't think about it, it was just a natural way of life in those days.

We moved into Lyon Street when I was about 7 (a big step nearer the sea).

The Olliver family. Between them they attended Nyewood School in Richmond Avenue for 57 years (note the school uniforms).

From right to left: Charles Jnr, Gwen, John, Phyllis, Reg, Betty (she died aged 12) and Ken.

Ken and I must have started school there at the same time but we cannot remember one another. We eventually met up in 1968.

Nyewood C of E School in Richmond Avenue. The foundation stone was laid in November 1898 and the first pupils admitted just two years later.

Nyewood C of E football team 1932/33. Charles Olliver Jnr is second from right (standing).

Nyewood C of E School: air-raid shelters stood by the playground during World War II.

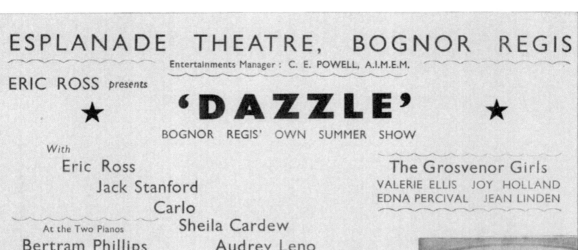

ESPLANADE THEATRE, BOGNOR REGIS

Entertainments Manager : C. E. POWELL, A.I.M.E.M.

ERIC ROSS presents

★ **'DAZZLE'** ★

BOGNOR REGIS' OWN SUMMER SHOW

With

Eric Ross

Jack Stanford

Carlo

At the Two Pianos **Sheila Cardew**

Bertram Phillips

and **Audrey Leno**

Eve White

Brenda Ross

John Gower

The Grosvenor Girls

VALERIE ELLIS   JOY HOLLAND
EDNA PERCIVAL   JEAN LINDEN

**WEEKDAYS at 8 p.m.   MATINEES, Wednesday and August Bank
Holiday Monday at 3 p.m.**   Prices 4/6, 3/6, 2/6 (Res.)   1/6 (Unres.)
Box Office Open   Children (except Saturdays and Bank Holiday Evenings)
Daily 10 a.m. to 8 p.m.   3/-, 2/-, 1/6 (Res.)   1/- (Unres.)

A programme from Bognor's Esplanade Theatre in the 1930s. Our Landlady (in Kenilworth Road) Eve White was one of the theatre pianists. She also played with her husband Billy in his Dance Band.

AT THE TWO PIANOS
BERTRAM PHILLIPS & EVE WHITE

Started his career at the age of 12 when he accompanied his father who was a singer. Ran his own show called 'Silver Dominoes' from 1939-46. Had a television engagement once a month in the old Savoy Hill days. Was composer and Musical Director for 12 years at the Pavilion Worthing. Joined Dazzle Cabaret in 1945.

Has had a wide experience in all branches of the musical profession. Played for several seasons in Ladies' Orchestra, including engagements at the Royal, Leamington Spa and Valley of Rocks Hotel, Lynton. Also had own orchestra.

During the war joined ENSA and toured the British Isles as pianiste to several well-known concert parties.

★

Esplanade Foyer

★

Band The Cameronians
(Scottish Rifles)
**18th to 31st JULY
Alamein Band of The Royal
Tank Regiment
1st to 29th AUGUST
Hotham Park Bandstand**

**12th July for 8 Weeks
Uncle Leslie
FAMILY FUNTIME**
Weekdays 11. am. 2.30 & 4 p.m.
**Eastern Esplanade
Bandstand**

BOGNOR REGIS FOR HEALTH.

G.A. NEAL & SONS FOR HOUSES.

THE PIER BOGNOR REGIS.

This postcard of Bognor Pier was actually a brochure from house bulders G.A. Neal & Sons contained a pull-out 'concertina' of tiny photographs showing off the features of the new houses that had just been built in North Bersted.

Mother and I at the gate of 'Junette' in Chichester Road c 1933. The picture was taken by a roving photographer (they used to call at houses for business).

The Rising Sun public house, also known as the 'Stamp House' because of its display of pictures and festoons made of postage stamps. Its name was later changed to 'Stamps' and it is now 'The Bersted Tavern'.

Festoons of stamps inside the back room of the pub.

With my parents in the back garden at Kenilworth Road.

The shopping parade in Aldwick Road in the 1930s.

The Princess Elizabeth Boating Pool opened in 1937. The pool was made in the shape of England and Wales (probably not enough room for Scotland!). Many a Bognor child landed in the pool attempting to jump from one port to another. The port names are now in the children's play area. The boating pool area is now the upper car park corner of Crescent Road and Canada Grove. Note the PIMCO store in the background (Portsea Island Mutual Co-operative – the 'Co-op').

Nyewood Lane in the 1930s. Note the two horse chestnut trees on the left.

On the move again…

The closest step we made to the seafront came in 1937 when we moved into 11 Lyon Street. My mother was in her element as we were in her newly-built modern home which was rented from the next-door neighbours at No 9. Our house was named 'Silverston' and theirs was 'Uley'.

Mother did summer letting from there and was always busy, particularly in 'Goodwood week', when the town was packed. Men would ask to sleep in the bath, on the landing or even under the stairs, as they preferred that to sleeping under the pier.

One lady who stayed with us was fascinated by the photograph in the hallway which portrayed the band of the 2nd Battalion Somerset Light Infantry. My father was a bass player in the band. She said, "The man pictured in the centre is my father!" My father was very pleased, as he had been fond of bandmaster James, who had been very caring. He had written the march 'Jelalabad' for the Somerset Light Infantry, to commemorate their battle there. With all the places in town she could have stayed, tt was amazing that she walked into our house!

The same families used to visit year after year and so became welcome friends, as witnessed by remarks in my parents' visitors book.

From a family in Tufnell Park N7: *"Six years of home from home 1933, 34, 35, 36, 37, 38. With our kindest thanks for your good welcome each year".*

A family from Rotherhythe wrote in August 1937 *"When thinking of Bognor we shall always remember and appreciate Mr and Mrs Knight."*

A thought-provoking entry from a family from Hayes in Kent, dated 25th – 30th May 1940 says, "Sorry to leave early, certainly not your fault!"

I believe that was the time when my father received his calling up papers for the army.

I remember the family from Tufnell Park; they first visited when we lived in Kenilworth Road. They were an engaged couple in 1933 and thereafter returned on honeymoon and then with their family in the latter years. As their names were Fred and Julie I promptly re-named them 'Punch and Judy'.

My father worked behind the bar at the Bedford Hotel on Saturday nights and played football on Saturday and Wednesday afternoons. I remember going around the corner every Saturday afternoon to buy him a packet of PK chewing gum before he went to football. I also remember the smell of the Elliman's linament he smeared on his legs and which my mother rubbed on his back. The charabanc used to pick us up in Crescent Road for away matches.

I used to fetch small items of shopping and would plead with mother to have some Mazawattee Tea, as they gave away different coloured sorbo balls with it. I must have had all the colours and I attempted to juggle with them.

Lyon Street School was a stone's throw away, so naturally I attended it. Miss Michie was the headmistress then. She was the sister of Brian Michie, who had a talent show on the radio. It was quite a strict School. I received the cane for laughing in class and also for taking a day off school to go on a steamer trip from the end of the pier (but it was worth it!).

The words of songs were explained to us, so that when we sang 'John Brown's Body', 'Pop Goes the Weasel', 'John Peel' etc, we knew the meaning of the song. Looking back it must have been innovative for its time.

Mrs Law had a shop opposite the school and many years later (in the late 1950s) when I returned to live in Lyon Street as a newly-married woman, she was still trading there and from her I learned the little-known fact that when boys buy gobstoppers they usually chose red ones. (My little son always preferred red sweets.)

The Laburnum Centre is now situated on the site of the old Lyon Street School.

*1934 was the first year of the 'Bognor Wednesdays'. They won the Sussex Mid-week Cup.
Back row (l to r) Cliff Wyatt, Billy King, Reg Andrews. Front row: Les Kingsbury, Alby Hammond*

Fred and Julie Morgan ('Punch & Judy') with me (sitting on the lap of a friend of Julie's sister). Julie's sister extreme right.

VIEW FROM WATERLOO GARDENS. BOGNOR REGIS.

My father always took me to Smith's in Waterloo Gardens on Saturday evenings, to buy me sweets.

"Sudley House"
Sudley Road
Bognor

RAMSDEN BROS PRINTERS WORTHING

A car park has now replaced this house in Lyon Street (it wrongly states SudleyRoad on the card).

Lyon Street School photographed in 1968. It was demolished in 1969.

I received the cane at Lyon Street School for staying away to go for a steamer trip to Worthing and back. Those were the days!

My Home Town

Oh! how fortunate I have been
The places In Bognor I have seen.
It had an air so genteel
I can almost touch it, it was so real.

The gracious buildings and the golden sand so fine
The sunny summer days they were mine.
Wooden steps leading up to reach
Bathing huts perched high on the beach.

Now the pebbles have really taken over
The lower walks waiting for time and tide to rediscover.
Along the seafront amusements to enjoy in the rain
Getting lost in the mirror maze - what a pain!

Brightly painted wooden clown heads turning from side to side
The exciting Ghost Train giving an eerie ride.
The Sunken Garden Cafe and Leslie's Cafe for tea,
Cream cakes at Polly Anne's, the height of propriety.

Those were the days of happy tea dances
St Bernard's Waltz and the Lancers
At the Coq D'or and the Picturedrome Hall,
Four Cinemas, three theatres; we had them all.

Roller skating, bands in the bandstand
Oh yes! Life was really grand!
Then later the Jitterbug and Jive
The Pavilion and Rex joyfully came alive.

Watching the Romain twins perform the 'Lemon Drop'.
The friendly greetings at the Village Hall' 'hop'.
Buckle and Clidero and Hawkes in the High Street
The pungent smell of Isteds was a treat.

Money was short but a good life was free
Many Bognorians will relate to my memory
For as I look around and at times feel down
I still feel privileged to have grown up
In Bognor Regis, my home town.

Sylvia Olliver, 10/1/1988

'Bathing huts perched high on the beach'.

ORCHESTRA ENCLOSURE, BOGNOR

'The lower walks waiting for time and tide to rediscover.'

The Sunken Garden Café.

'Amusements to enjoy in the rain.'

Leslie's café can be seen on the opposite side of the road beyond Reynolds. The sign is next to the branches of small tree.

A band in the bandstand entertains onlookers c1920.

'The Pavilion and Rex really came alive."

Hawkes in the High Strret.

'The pungent smell of Isted's.'

Memories of Bognor Regis & Chichester in the 30s, 40s & 50s

The Esplanade Theatre

The Theatre Royal cinema.

PIER THEATRE

BOGNOR REGIS   'Phone 575

SUNDAY, AUGUST 24th, at 8 p.m.

LESLIE NEWPORT presents

THE
BIG SHOW

IN AID OF THE

NORTH DEVON
FLOOD DISASTER FUND

★ ALL STAR PROGRAMME ★
OF WELL-KNOWN ARTISTES

POPULAR PRICES : 2/6, 3/6, 4/6

COME and HELP This Worthy Cause

Jennings'—The Printers, Bognor Regis.

8343

PIER THEATRE

BOGNOR REGIS   -   'PHONE 575

Licensee and Manager   Claude K. Fuds

★

LESLIE NEWPORT

presents

"SUMMERTIME"

1952
EDITION

★

Nightly at 8

Matinees (if wet) at 2.30

Souvenir Programme No. 2 . Price 6d.

Jennings'—The Printers, West Street, Bognor Regis

'Four cinemas, three theatres; we had them all.'

SOUVENIR PROGRAMME

GRAND OPENING OF

THE ODEON THEATRE
BOGNOR REGIS

14TH JULY. 1934

A Town of Character

The town of my childhood was a place of aromas: the smell of freshly ground coffee from Buckle and Clidero & Hawkes in the High Street; the many pungent smells from Isted's next to Woolworths in London Road. They seemed to sell everything: corn, pet food, straw, delicatessen, flower pots etc.

Then came the arrival of Marks and Spencers with a café in the rear left-hand corner of the store.

Woolworths had a Tea-bar around the rear right-hand corner, the counters stocked with many items including biscuits displayed in their slightly tipped tins. Broken biscuits, sold in paper bags, were good value.

A bucket of sand and a bucket of water were placed behind the counters in case of fire. I learned of this in 1951 when I noticed a dog walking into Woolworths at 9 am when they opened. He walked behind the counter and drank out of the fire bucket. When I commented on this I was told that he did so every morning at the same time when he was out for his walk.

Next to Marks & Spencer was a small coal merchants where they displayed a huge, shiny lump of coal.

It was in this vicinity that a roving photographer took holiday snaps.

Lemmon's was situated next to Woolworth's; they sold clothes, bed linen, haberdashery etc. Payment was put into a container which travelled along a rail to the cashier, who returned the change in the same manner.

A little shoe shop opposite St John's Church (now replaced by Boots and WH Smith's) somewhat curiously also sold budgerigars, as the owner bred them. My father bought his budgies there, as we had an aviary. Afterwards a Baker took over the shop. I wonder if he sold seed cake?

The water tower next to St John's Church was demolished and a row of shops with flats above was built. Shirley's department store was one of the newly built shops. I coveted one of the big baby dolls which they were selling at five shillings each. I was thrilled when I received one for Christmas.

Other businesses in town included Colborn and Wingate, bakers in the High Street, Peter Derry's the bakers in Station Road, the Coq d'Or Restaurant next to the Odeon cinema and the Picturedrome all had rooms above which could be used for tea dances and social gatherings.

Bognor children had a choice of entertainment on Saturday mornings; roller skating at the Pavilion or Saturday morning pictures at the Odeon. The child who took the most used postage stamps to the Saturday morning picture show would receive a box of Maltesers, a real treat when pocket money was a penny a week. I won it one week and was in seventh heaven.

We seemed to know the majority of people then, perhaps because my father played football for the town and played in the British Legion band. It was such a friendly town and whenever we went out walking we were constantly stopping to talk. A number of my friends lived above the town shops.

Unfortunately all this was put on hold and never properly regained for me and many thousands of other people when the Second World War was declared and altered our lives forever – but that's another story.

Timothy Whites on the left, Staley's on the right with Pinks the provision store further down. The 'P' is still on the front of the building.

Two views of Bognor Regis High Street in the 1950s (top) and the 1920s (bottom).

Bognor High Street in the 1950s

The Southdown bus station

The impressive fleet vehicles belonging to Lewis and Co, the removal firm, parked in Sudley Road..

London Road in the 1950s.

Sudley Road, as it was in the 1930s – completely devoid of cars!

St John's church in London Road.

c1930. Bognor taxi drivers wait for the bride behind St John's church in Sudley Road. Charles Olliver Snr is 2ⁿᵈ from right.
This was a time when taxi drivers would knock on doors on arrival, would open the taxi door for their customers and wore uniforms!
Note the lady driver 3ʳᵈ from left – the first lady taxi driver in Bognor Regis.

Charles Olliver Snr, who had been a submariner in World War I, photographed in diving gear before laying the first sewage pipe out to sea from an area that is now part of Butlin's, but which was then an area used as a coach park and sewage farm.

Bognor Regis Boy's Brigade in 1932/3

Back row: Jack Steer, Vic ?, Jack Tate, Alan Robinson, Wally Lawrence, and Stan Hawkins, ? Balchin, Phil Creacy.

2nd row: Frank Hackett, Arthur Joy, Fred Allan, Fred Terry, Charles Olliver Jr, Gordon Young, Don Sheppard, Len Sheppard, Wally Prior, Eric Steer, unknown, Jack Smurthwaite.

3rd row: Ash Baker, Harry Holloway, Les Wyeth, ? Ridges, unknown, Frank Wyeth, Reg Irish, Bill Reed.

Front row: unknown, ? Calcut, ? Gibbs, Ron Young, unknown, ? Richards, Norman Steer.

In 1939 my class at Lyon Street School was taken by train to Southampton docks to look over the Empress of Britain. I recently learned that this ship was sunk during the Second World War. We then travelled on to Winchester to look over the cathedral. It was a happy day and I remember how exciting it all was.

Flint Cottage

Flint Cottage with rooms of memory for me,
The days of childhood, adolescence and maybe,
My 'featherbed grandma' so loving and caring,
What little she had was always for sharing.

Photographs arranged and filling the front room table
Looking at them, guess what? We were able
To know which aunts and uncles were coming to call,
For their photos were put at the front to see from the hall.
The picture of Granddad in First World War uniform
Looking gaunt and proud in fur coat, well trench-worn
It took pride of place on the sitting room wall.
A fine figure of a man over six feet tall.

The fireplace where chestnuts were set to go 'pop'!
As out from the fire they shot – "Don't touch, too hot!"
Visiting grandchildren vying to please and placate
As the table legs and cupboard door they tried to negotiate
Crawling under the table, if I was the winner
Ten pennies in the gas meter for cooking the Sunday dinner.

Grandma whitening the stone step every day,
Inside the cottage, I really must say.
It leads down into the back room from the hall,
The living room with a view of the North Wall.
The room where on Sunday afternoons with a jug of shandy,
A basin of winkles on the table, a pin each – that was handy!
Newmarket at tuppence halfpenny a time in the kitty
Would I win this time? Oh! What a pity!
Granddad sitting in his chair like a lord
With matchsticks ready by the crib board.
I tried but never understood the game
But liked to hear him say "one for his nob!" just the same.

The stone copper in the corner of the scullery,
The memory brings wonderful odours to me
Of washing and Monday dinnertime stew
And suet pudding with lots of syrup too.
The outside lavatory with wooden seat scrubbed white
I never used to venture out there late at night.
One of my uncles had written "The Ritz" on the door
If the Ritz smelt like that, I was glad I was poor!

Sitting in the front bedroom where I was born
Watching Granddad in bed and feeling very forlorn
For he was dying and had been ill for a year
What was dying? Was it something to fear?
Caught him looking at me with eyes sunken in pain
Oh Granddad! I wish I had our time again,
I was only 14 when you passed away.
I wish we had really known one another to say
All the unspoken thoughts we innermost feel
But cannot communicate or bare and reveal.
Grandmother taken ill after Granddad had died
Sleeping with her, feeling comfortable by her side.
The feather mattress she pummelled every day
She would not let anyone else do it – that was her way

The little Dutch girl ornament dressed in orange and white
She swayed from side to side – "touch her gently, she's very light!"
She sat on the bedroom mantleshelf, gazing coyly at the bed
Now I remember, she also moved her head.
Brass bedstead with one knob turning around
Who knows if it came off what might be found?

Three sons and sons-in-law, boyfriends always welcome
Six daughters, daughters-in-law, girlfriends always made "at home".
Nineteen grandchildren, all loved in every way
A card received by everyone on their birthday.
Peacetime, wartime, peacetime again,
All the different uniforms proudly worn by the men.
One son missing – all gathering there,

Good news telegram arrived – no more tears to spare.

Grandma died a number of years ago
But, dearest Grandma, I'm glad I was born to your 'Flo',
And whenever I pass that Flint cottage door
I'm proud to say "I was born at 204."

Sylvia Olliver, July 1983

Grandma with Brian and Sylvia.

Mum on the right, Grandma, and Uncle Albert's wife Edith on the left.

Granddad in First World War uniform and fur coat.

Uncle Albert Daniels in navy uniform. He was serving on the Afridi when it was sunk. There were only six survivors; he was one of the fortunate six. Before joining the navy he attended Oliver Whitby's Bluecoat School, which was in a building now part of the Army & Navy department store in West Street Chichester.

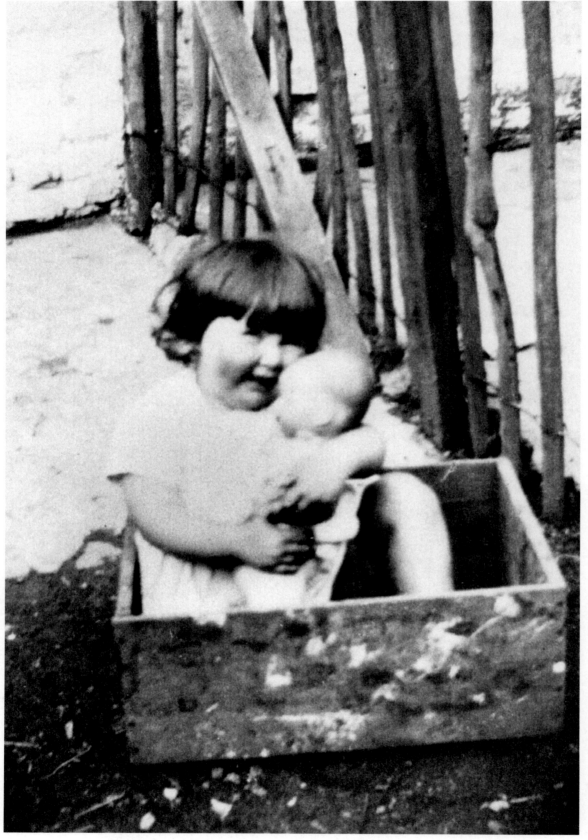

Sylvia cuddling her doll in a wooden box in the backyard of 204 Orchard Street , Chichester.

On Bonfire night Grandma would tie sparklers and Catherine wheels to the tops of the fencing you can see behind me and we would have jumping Jack crackers. I can still smell the nose-twitching memory now!

Memories of Chichester

The friendly atmosphere of Chichester has changed greatly over the years since it has become "upmarket". During the 1930s and 40s it had the feel of the city but was divided into a number of smaller communities, each one having its own distinct character with a corner shop, a pub and a local hall where such things as whist and beetle drives were held.

Orchard Street, situated at the Northgate end of Chichester, was just such a street, with Lambourne's shop on the corner with Chapel Street. The owner would be alerted that a customer was calling by the tinkling of a bell which rang as the door was opened. You would go down into the front room of the house which had been converted into a shop with a counter on the left, complete with scales. Sacks of sugar and dry goods filled the floor. The dry goods were all weighed into stiff, dark blue bags. I mustn't forget Tizer; it was the children's favourite drink at the time!

Mrs Lambourne knew all the families down the road, so we only had to ask for the items to be put on Grandma's bill (with her permission of course) and it would be paid at the end of the week.

The 'Nursery Arms' pub was situated on the other corner of Chapel Street. It was there that Granddad spent many an evening playing crib with his cronies. The Nursery Arms is no longer a pub and is now a private house. Across the road at the corner of Orchard Avenue there used to be a baker's; it is now hairdressers.

The Salvation Army citadel is still situated down Orchard Street (but in 2003 is for sale). I always ran out to watch the parade on Sundays; it was wonderful to hear the band playing as they joyfully marched down the street.

My grandparents had a wireless set and if the accumulator (battery) needed recharging while I was visiting I would be asked to take it to the garage next to Bartholomew's (the corn merchant's) to be recharged, but always warned to be careful not to spill it; it was filled with acid and could burn.

Milk was delivered and measured out of churns at the doorstep. Bread was delivered every day and visiting grandchildren, myself included, all wanted the small round top of the cottage loaf.

We could buy home-made ice cream from a house at the Northgate end of the street (was it the Janeece's at No 9?). An Italian family lived there and the man used to ride his bicycle with the ice cream container with the usual entreaty to "stop me and by one".

Opposite their house, where Metro House is now situated, was spare land. The White Horse Inn had previously been there but had burnt down in the late 1930s. I can't remember what, if anything, other than a small hut stood on the spare land as my main concern was selling my grandma's jam jars to the man in the hut so that I could go to the pictures. A few coppers went a long way in those days!

There was a large outbuilding at the bottom of my grandparent's garden where Uncle Ron looked after sick birds and wild animals. People were always knocking on the door handing over injured animals and birds for him to look after.

Grandma kept chickens which were quite fortunate as corn from the corn merchant's two doors away often blew into the garden. When I stayed there, one of the comforting sounds was the sound of the cock crowing in the morning.

The city also had the usual well-known food stores: Lipton's, the International, David Greig's, Maypole Dairy, Macfisheries, Elphick's the pork butchers, Home & Colonial. There was also Fielders the newsagents and Bunns the greengrocers at the corner of Baffins Lane. All of the foregoing were in East Street.

I must not forget Shippam's sausages – Oh, the aroma and the taste! I have never found any comparable. During the war we queued for ages to buy just one pound of them. The recipe was a secret; if only it could be found and revived!

Michael Guarnaccio – 'Mickey' to everyone – was a well-known character. He had a small shop at the Northgate end of North Street, so consequently knew my family, including all 19 grandchildren. He must have been puzzled by my request on one occasion for two shillings worth of Rizla cigarette papers which I bought for Granddad's birthday. I hadn't realised just how many papers were in each pack, but I remember how proud I was to give them to Granddad (he must have been amused).

Almost opposite Mickey's was another sweet shop, next to a fish and chip shop.

The city's three cinemas, the Corn Exchange and the Gaumont in East Street and the Plaza (later renamed the Odeon) in South Street must bring back many memories to people of my age group who grew up in Chichester. Boys would wolf whistle at the girls in those days and although at times we pretended not to hear, I am sure that the majority of us enjoyed the attention!

Sloe Fair Day was a day to remember. Was it because I was a child that I remember the atmosphere as one of excitement and colour and joy and exuberance of all who were there? The sheer vitality of the fair was a young person's heaven. Do today's children and teenagers view it with such gusto, I wonder? Will they remember the annual event in 60 years time as if it were yesterday? I certainly hope so. Fairs were also held on the land where Rowes Garage was later situated in the Hornet.

My uncle George was always very annoyed to hear people call the Sloe Fair area 'the Festival Theatre carpark'. He used to say, "It is Sloe Fair Field, left to the people of Chichester for the Sloe Fair hundreds of years before the Festival Theatre was built!"

My mother was born in Cooper Street in 1909 so was a true Cicestrian, having been born within the four walls of Chichester. Her family also lived in Little London and then Fishbourne for awhile, living down Mill Lane at Salt Mill House, so she attended school there and later on returned to Chichester to Orchard Street, where she attended school in Chapel Street. She told me that she used to write on a slate with chalk.

My parents were married in St Paul's Church, just around the corner from her family home. I was also christened there and my son John was confirmed there.

The tranquillity of the fair city of Chichester was disturbed by the invasion of Canadian troops during the last war. Their unusual pastime of crouching on street corners rolling dice and their madcap ways thoroughly bemused me as a young girl.

The afternoon and the evening before the Dieppe raid saw the Canadian soldiers walking around Chichester in their camouflage outfits with blackened faces. My Granddad, who had served in the trenches during the First World War, commented with a few expletives, that it was stupid as anyone could see that they were prepared to go overseas and that this news would be sure to reach the Germans, who would be waiting for them. How right he was! I often wonder how many of those jaunty young men ever saw their homeland again. Subsequently, German aircraft flew over Chichester and dropped leaflets showing photographs of the Canadians they had captured during the Dieppe raid – it was very sad to see them.

Granddad always insisted on listening to Lord Haw-Haw on the wireless. He used to get very irate listening to this traitor, especially when he announced that 'Bognor Regis Harbour' had been bombed! Lord Haw-Haw was really William Joyce and was used by the Germans to try to demoralise us. After the war he was imprisoned and sentenced to death as a traitor.

Mum and I were on a number 57 bus from Bognor to Chichester when we saw in the distance a German bomber diving over the Chichester area and bombs raining down. We were very worried, wondering whether our family would be safe. On arrival we were relieved to find that they were safe, although we found North Street had been hit. The Crooked S was badly damaged all the way through from St Martin's to North Street. Auntie Audrey worked at Penneys, next to the Assembly Rooms, and had been knocked down the steps from the haberdashery department into the millinery department. A number of people were killed and injured that day.

It was a family joke that when Granddad and his friend Mr Blyton, who lived two doors away, got together discussing their memories of the time they spent in the trenches, it sounded as if the two of them had won the war together. I now wish that I had overheard their conversations, it would have given me more of an insight into the horrors of trench warfare.

Exterior and interior views of St Bartholemew's Chichester.

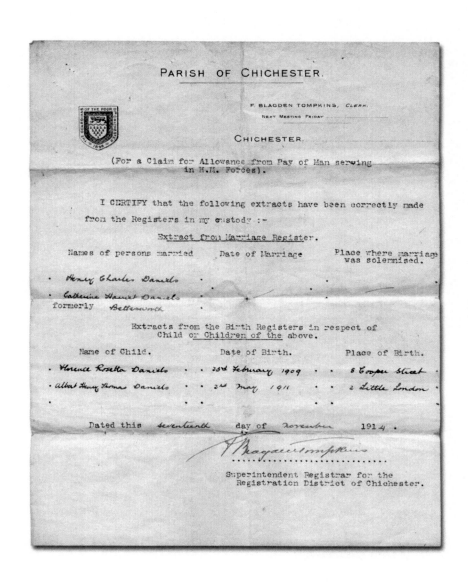

PARISH OF CHICHESTER.

F. BLAGDEN TOMPKINS, *Clerk.*

Next Meeting Friday _____

CHICHESTER. _____

(For a Claim for Allowance from Pay of Man serving
in H.M. Forces).

I CERTIFY that the following extracts have been correctly made
from the Registers in my custody :-

Extract from Marriage Register.

Names of persons married	Date of Marriage	Place where marriage was solemnised.
Henry Charles Daniels		
Catherine Harriet Daniels formerly Betteworth		

Extracts from the Birth Registers in respect of
Child or Children of the above.

Name of Child.	Date of Birth.	Place of Birth.
Florence Rosetta Daniels	25th February, 1909	5 Cooper Street
Albert Henry Thomas Daniels	2nd May 1911	2 Little London

Dated this *seventeenth* day of *November* 1914.

....

Superintendent Registrar for the
Registration District of Chichester.

My grandparents' claim for Army allowance and my Mother's confirmation card.

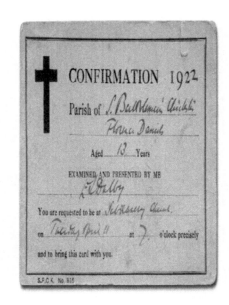

CONFIRMATION 1922

Parish of _____

Florence Daniels

Aged 13 Years

EXAMINED AND PRESENTED BY ME

_____

You are requested to be at _____

on _____ at _____ o'clock precisely

and to bring this card with you.

S.P.C.K. No. 815

Frederick Hill Builders Ltd, Nothgate, Chichester. My Granddad, Henry Charles (Harry) Daniels is 3rd from right, wearing a Trilby.

Uncle Ron (centre, left hand photo) and friends outside the Nursery Arms pub.

(above left) My Mother, Florence Rosetta Knight (née Daniels) with me c 1930 in the back garden of my grandparents home at 204 Orchard Street. (above right) Auntie Ella takes a ride down Orchard Street in a motor car c 1930.

My son John was 1 year and 4 months old in 1956 when her Majesty the Queen visited Chichester. I caught the 31 bus from Bognor Regis complete with son and pushchair and watched the Queen and Prince Philip arrive at St Pancras from Goodwood and later saw them again in Priory Park.

Chichester's Mayor receiving the Duchess of York in the late 1920s or early 1930s.

Chichester market cross wore Gala dress from 18th to 30th December 1930 (left). East Street in the late 40s (right).

This postcard was posted in December 1947. Note the horse chestnut tree close to the Corn Exchange, now sadly missing from East Street but fondly remembered by many.

This postcard was posted in October 1949 but it would appear that the photograph was taken during World War II: note the soldiers on bicycles, also the Regnum Tea Rooms and Maypole Stores signs on the left.

East Street in the 1950s. Note the Tudor Café on the left and further down the sign for Pallant Tearooms – both very popular.

Chichester's famous Market Cross as seen from East Street. Note the policeman on duty. Also note Barrett's the bookseller stationer and newsagent on the corner of South Street which had to be demolished.

An aerial view of the Market Cross in the late 1920s/early 1930s shows the higgledy-piggledy rooftops characteristic of Chichester.

East Street in the 1940s. Note the International Stores on the left.

South Street in the 1930s. Note the opticians sign on the right.

South Street in 1949. Note Boots the Chemist on the left.

South Street in the 1950s

North Street in the 1920s.

North Street in 1956.

This postcard of North Street shows the tower of St Peter the Less (centre) which was demolished in 1957.

Westgate, Chichester 60566

These two postcards show houses in West Street that were demolished to make way for a roundabout.

View from the Bell Tower, Chichester.

Tower Street, Chichester

I well remember Tower Street as depicted in these two picture postcards. The Grange wall and gates on the left were demolished and the grounds now house County Hall and its car park. Note the steps up to the North walls at the far end of the street.

Tower Street, Chichester

Ladies parade down South Street, Chichester. Note Morants (now the Army & Navy) in the background. The date and purpose of the parade are unknown.

An aerial view of Southgate, Chichester in the 1930s.

The Lancastrian County Secondary School for Boys, Chichester when newly opened in the 1950s.

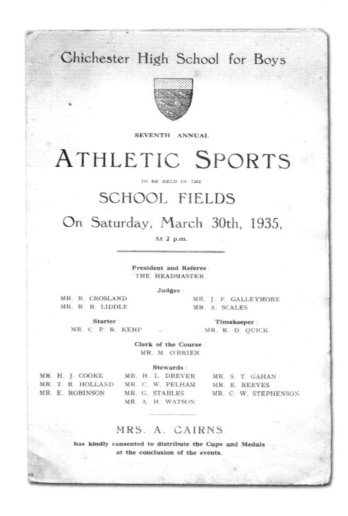

Sports day programme of Chichester High School for Boys.

this photograph was taken on 5th May 1936. The sign on the lorry tells the story.

Two photographs from a Shippham's brochure produced in 1952 show what it was like inside the factory.

Specialities for Xmas.

SOUPS.

SAUSAGES.

The Best Sausages Made.

Tins and Glasses.

1 lb. Boxes, 8/- doz.

Shippam, Chichester.

PRICE LIST.

Specialities for Christmas Trade.

At Christmas time.

From time immemorial Yuletide is associated with plentiful and dainty fare.

Christmas Fare and merry-making would not be complete without the show dishes.

To ensure good digestion wait on appetite, and health on both may prove true.

Buy...

SHIPPAM'S SPECIALITIES FOR XMAS.

Christmas Fare.

Food & Cookery.

"Shippam, Chichester, has introduced a delicious pudding, which it would be hard to beat as regards the richness and flavour, and can be recommended as being of first-rate quality."

Finest Quality Ingredients used only.

Plum Puddings (in Basins).

No. 1 size, about 1 lb., each packed in box, per doz.				**8/3**
,, 2 ,,	2 lb.,	,,	,,	**15/-**
,, 3 ,,	3 lb.,	,,	,,	**22/-**
,, 4 ,,	4 lb.,	,,	,,	**30/-**

Breakfast.	SAUSAGES	per doz.	**8/-**
	WILD BOAR'S HEAD (in glass)	,,	**10/-**
	BRAWN (in glass)	,,	**10/-**
Luncheon.	OX TONGUES (in glass)	,,	**33/-**
	CURRIED CHICKEN, per doz.	9/- and	**12/-**
	GALANTINES (in glass)	from	**8/3**
	PRESSED BEEF	,,	**16/-**
Tea	POTTED MEATS	,,	**5/-**
	FISH PASTES	,,	**5/-**
Dinner.	SOUPS (tins and glass)	from	**6/-**
	SAUSAGE MEAT for Stuffing 1 lb. boxes		**8/-**

Shippams Xmas price list, date unknown.

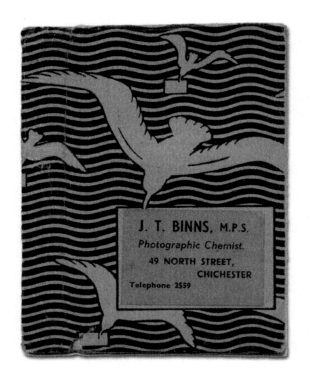

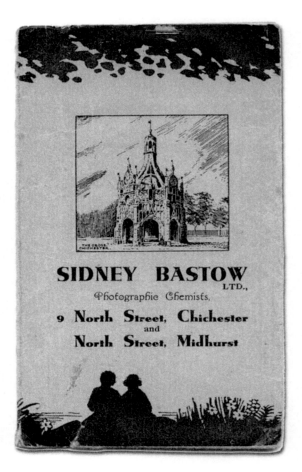

Photo wallets from some of Chichester's photography specialists.

A Wartime Poem

What did the war years mean to me when
The heart racing noise of the first air raid siren
Sounded one September Sunday morning
Without any frightening prior warning
Sending us all fleeing unaware of any tangible outcome for the stairs
To sit under the houses safest place
Oh God! What had happened to the human race?

Later the Battle of Britain going on overhead - bravery now retold
Of actions and men so brave and bold
The tracery overhead in the skies
As allied airmen fought German for the ultimate prize,
The red glow as Portsmouth burned at night
Our firemen racing there to help at another dastardly sight,

A school friend's father taken prisoner of war
How long before my dad would be a soldier once more?
Eleven years on reserve finished six weeks before war began
Wouldn't be long before he would have to be a king's man,
The comforting sight of his double bass under my bed
As I knelt at the side and my nightly prayers said,
And then having to hand it back to the British Legion band
Meant that my dad was wearing khaki for his land.

Leaving my little bedroom for my mum's double one
Knowing that like me her little world had broken down,
Saying my prayers with more feeling and fervour than before
"Please God bless everyone and bring my dad back safely from war."

The evacuees sitting waiting in the railway station nearby
Then walking through the streets watched by not many a dry eye,
Some with their mothers and some all alone
"Any room in the inn?" - wanting a home,
Made me feel guilty for feeling sad
Worrying about mum and missing my dad.

Hit and run raiders as over the sea they hopped

The air raid siren often sounding as the bombs dropped,

Going to the Odeon to see Walt Disney's Pinocchio

A sign flashed on the screen - 'the siren has sounded, off home you can go'

'Look after your ticket you can get back in,'

Running all the way home to the sirens wailing din,

Singing the Marseillaise and "For those in peril on the sea"

Also "There'll always be an England" in school assembly

Going to school one week mornings the next afternoons

That was looked on by the children as one of war time's boons,

Finding out that it was difficult for mum to pay her way

Trying to live on a serviceman's meagre army pay,

Then we had to sally forth

For mum to do war work up north

Sub letting our home to an airman's family

Leaving my school and grandparents dear to me,

Travelling on noisy steam trains to places new

And nearly always having a long wait at Crewe.

Standing or sitting in corridors of trains jam-packed

With all our bones feeling as if they were cracked,

To live in a strange Yorkshire town

For Mum to work at David Brown's.

The only southerner at Berry Brow School

At eleven years old trying to prove I wasn't a southern fool,

The headmaster by name Hiram Whitwam

A rather gruff, but kindly ex-naval man,

Told me to stand up for myself and fight back

Something that later I was glad I didn't lack.

Ashby-de-la-Zouche, Heckmondwyke, Thornton Moor

Numerous places Dad stationed there

A weekend - more unknown faces,

Leaving Huddersfield on a Friday at midnight
To travel back down south
Grandma's house a lovely sight,

On Sunday night back we would go
Making me feel very homesick and low,
Crossing London on the Underground
People huddled on the platforms to escape the sound
Of the Blitz erupting overhead
Anywhere to lay down, making a bed,

A sleepless night travelling - mum straight to work
Me off to school - war time - we didn't shirk
Then in August 1942, a lot of sorting out to do,
For the RAF man's family had left our home
We had to get it ready to make someone else welcome.

On August 14th a Heinkel 111 flew low
With machine guns blazing made terror grow,
Talking to a lady in the back garden only fifteen minutes before
That German bomber making her another statistic of war.

We had gone around the corner into town
Went back to find it had all been bomb blasted down,
No one present had seen us leave
The searchers cheered with relief,

It was all a terrible sight
Flats, houses destroyed by the bomb's might,
People looking dazed and scared it was all like a dreadful nightmare,
What was salvaged was put into store
Our home at 11 Lyon Street existed no more.

Tough little evacuees sent up to Yorkshire from Kent
Buzz bombs so deadly frightening - their lives were rent,
Southerners together we did unite
In the playground the Northerners to fight,

Dad stationed at Southampton in June 44
Street after street packed with the vehicles of war,
GI's waiting to embark for they knew not where
Giving away life saver sweets they had to spare.

After the weekend going back up north
Keeping quiet for all we were worth,
June 6th was the famous D-Day
Our men landing on strange beaches far away,
Our thoughts and hearts were with them all the time
Later i was worried about dad's ship being struck by a mine,
He had told me to keep quiet and not tell anyone
That he was with the men going over to bring the POWs back from Belgium.
He said it was a terrible sight and the smell as well
The prisoners and the boats stank like hell,

We travelled down to Southampton, stayed right near the compound
A horrible raw snowy day with POWs all around,
A motley crowd as they marched through the gate
Children hurling snowballs at them in their hate.

Then in November just after his 66th birthday
My dearest Granddad in Chichester passed away.
We all gathered for the funeral at 204
Another episode of changing life touching that door.

The smell of chrysanthemums was pungent and pervading
A constant reminder of that sad day never fading,
Returning up north, mum not feeling well
As it turned out it was our last spell,
For mum had a heart attack at the age of thirty-five
We had to return south for her to stay alive,
War work and rheumatic fever at twenty one had left its mark
And could not be undone,
So grandma made us welcome once more
As we awaited that happy ending of the war,

Then, on that never-to-be-forgotten 8th May

We celebrated Victory in Europe day,

Gathering in Chichester's market place

Servicemen and civilians in one huge embrace,

Relief and thankfulness tinged with sadness

For widows and orphans not enjoying full gladness,

So we awaited the final day of war

When victory in Japan day arrived we danced and prayed once more.

Then after all the years mum and I had had to roam

We had to hunt and hunt to try to find a home,

Eventually we had a place requisitioned for us

After we had had to make a fuss,

Bombed out and nowhere to go.

Why did we still have to fight so?

Dad was not demobbed straight away

We had to wait until late 1946 for that day,

Grey and white pin stripe suits galore

Thank god for the men and women safely home from war.

Dad (left), Uncle Ron Daniels (centre) and Uncles Albert & George (Snowy) Daniels in wartime uniform.

This photograph of myself and Mother was taken for Dad when he enlisted for Army service in 1940. Dresses were bought from Lemmons. Mine was pink and white, Mum's navy blue and white.

November 1944. My aunts Audrey on the left and Vera on the right, placing flowers on Granddad's grave on their wedding day. Uncle Bunny Jackson on left; Uncle Reg Dolan on right.

Grandma and Granddad had six daughters and three sons. Their three sons were in the Navy the Royal Air Force and the Army. Their eldest daughter had one son and one daughter in the services. Their four other daughters had husbands in the services. One daughter was a WAAF and her husband in the Army.

Bognor children play with the remains of a Junkers 87 that crashed near Felpham.

Citizens of Bognor Regis celebrate VE-Day.

Yorkshire

We went up to Yorkshire in September 1941, just days before my 11th birthday. To leave my home, school, grandparents and Bognor Regis my lovely home town, was such a wrench – plus the fact that I had never travelled further than Plymouth to the West or London to the North. The train journey up to Yorkshire seemed never-ending. My mother was 32 years old, so it must have been quite a brave venture for her to undertake in those days.

When we finally arrived at Huddersfield's imposing station, we walked across the large square to catch a trolleybus to Lockwood. On alighting we were faced by a very steep hill with a roughly built wall to the right. I remember thinking "What are we doing here?" "Why are we here?" and "I wonder what's at the top?" Whatever was there would be our life for a long, long time. It was almost as if we were climbing to our unknown future.

At the top and we were confronted by a chapel, a Co-op, a fish and chip hut and rows and rows of terraced houses with the mill chimney towering in the background. It was entirely alien to everything I had seen in my life before.

Dad was stationed close-by and had booked us into one of the houses. We met the owner, who was a rather stern lady who, much to my interest, did not have any eyebrows. We did not stay there very long. Later on, a girl who lived opposite informed me that her family was not surprised that we had not stayed long; a previous army family had found it very difficult to share a house with this particular lady, as she did not want the husband and wife to have any time together there.

I settled into the school about one and a half miles away at Berry Brow. When the headmaster Mr Hyram Whitwam found out that the Saturday we had travelled to Yorkshire was the day I should have sat my high school exam (I had already passed the preliminary examination) he set the exam for me in his study. I passed, and therefore qualified for Greenhead High School, but to his chagrin I chose to stay at Berry Brow where I was beginning to make new friendships. Given that I had just undergone the greatest change of my life, leaving everyone and everything I had ever known, plus the fact that my mother was now out all day at work, my father was in the Army and we were now living in just a bedroom instead of a house, I felt I had enough for me to cope with. I have since regretted that decision, but after all, I was only just 11 years old. By the time I was fourteen and had been entered for Huddersfield Polytechnic, my mother was ill and we were returning back down south.

During the three years we spent in Yorkshire, we moved in and around Huddersfield six times. Only once did we have a bed sitting room with a fireplace; unfortunately it was down to the owner of the house to let us buy some of their coal ration, as one home could not have double the amount or even slightly more, even if there was more than one family living in the house. When we did manage to elicit some coal, I felt quite guilty. It was down to me to light the fire before my mother came home from work; not always an easy job.

My happiest time there was spent in one of the group of four houses where the owners had a son. The husband would play Monopoly and was very kind to me. His wife was very worried about a possible invasion and showed me a bottle of peroxide she would use on her own and her son's hair to bleach it, as it had been said that the Germans would kill anyone who did not have Aryan colouring. She then showed me an injection needle she would use if the subterfuge of the peroxide didn't work. It quite worried me at the time, being a subject I had not heard discussed before. Looking back, it must have been her way of coping with the unknown. She was normally such a bundle of fun.

The Yorkshire countryside looked so different to a Southerner but I quite liked the dry stone walls which separated the fields. It was quite disorientating to a girl who had grown up by the sea to realise that I could now travel in every direction, whereas in Bognor Regis it had always been West, East or North; now I could travel south as well.

The young people of the area belonged to the Methodist Christian Endeavourers (I still have my CE badge). We would meet up for social events and often walked in the surrounding countryside, marching along singing "I'm H.A.P.P.Y." etc. Honley and Holmfirth were favourite places, where one could enjoy the countryside depicted in "Last of the Summer Wine". There was also the Whitsun walk, when all the children of the area would wear their best clothes and walk around the village. The adults would gather to watch them walk past. It was quite a problem to find so-called "best clothes" during wartime and in fact, for a time afterwards, as clothing coupons had to be used for everything, even shoes, I used to wear dresses I had grown out of under my gymslip for extra warmth; the top looked like a blouse.

Snow in the winter months was, and is, the norm for Yorkshire, so Wellington boots were a must, also a spade was always kept indoors to dig a way out of the door. We used to sit in school in our coats, as there wasn't any heating. One year, nearly all the children in my class went down with yellow jaundice. I started it. I think it was the fact that we were so cold all the time. A child sitting in front of me turned around and noticed that the whites of my eyes were yellow. No wonder I had been feeling ill and tired; subsequently I spent a few weeks away from school.

It was during my six weeks school holiday, spent back in Sussex staying with my grandma in August 1942 that our home in Bognor was bombed. My father had a week's leave and came down to get the garden back into shape. He travelled down with me and then mother came down to clean the house through before new tenants replaced the RAF couple who had been renting it while we were away in Huddersfield. She sent the weekly rent difference to our landlady and landlords who lived next door. The day she finished and the day before we were to return to Huddersfield, the bomb dropped!

I returned to Huddersfield in 1975 and again in 1995 for a holiday, to find that the Methodist chapel was now not used, the mill had closed and the Co-op and fish and chip shop had disappeared. The only place still in use in that area that I remembered was the working men's club.

The old indoor market in Huddersfield where we used to queue for the "drink to cure all ills" had been demolished, and new modern market had taken its place, but it did not have the same atmosphere.

The Author, aged 12. Taken at Berry Brow School, Huddersfield, Yorkshire during World War 2.

The deep snow of a typical Yorkshire winter was something of a novelty for a girl from the South.
I am pictured here whilst recuperating from yellow jaundice.

It was from Lockwood that we climbed up the steep road and caught our first sight of Huddersfield. The mill chimney and chapel are easily seen. My mother and I stayed just along from the chapel at Taylor Hill. My school at Berry Brow was a walk to the top right. A cricket ground was situated next to the viaduct, but when I last visited in 1995 it was very overgrown and impassable.

Berry Brow, where I attended school from September 1941 to September 1944.
Castle Hill overlooks the area; I often walked there on Sundays.

The Doll's House that saved my life

The Victorian doll's house complete with furniture, little plant pots in the window, tiny candlesticks and miniature fittings, would today command a high price, but although the only tangible reminder I have left is one tiny candlestick, to me that doll's house was priceless.

It came into my life when I was about four. At that time my father was a milkman and would often come home with small gifts for me given to him by his customers. On that particular day I was waiting for him as usual in the back garden of our house, three houses away from the twitten which leads into Hawthorn Road, Bognor Regis. He was having great difficulty pushing his bike as he had the doll's house placed on top.

I saw him in the twitten across the back gardens and excitedly rushed indoors to tell my mother that Dad had a doll's house for me. What hours of pleasure I had with that house! Rearranging the furniture and inventing a pretend family to live in it brought me so much joy.

The years passed, we moved into Lyon Street, the war came and our world was turned upside down, along with millions of others. Dad was called up for the army in 1940. Mum and I were visiting Grandma's in Chichester on August 13th 1942 when an aunt called in and asked if I would give my dolls house to my cousin, who was a few years younger than me. We arranged there and then to put it on a No 31 bus at Bognor Regis bus station next afternoon at a prearranged time so she could be there to collect it when it arrived at Chichester.

The following afternoon I was in our back garden in Lyon Street, which backed onto a tall house of three flats fronting onto Sudley Road. Each flat had a door leading out onto a platform with an iron staircase which zigzagged up the back.

Mrs Grapes lived in the second flat and was on her section talking down to me. I told her that I was going to the bus station and asked her if she wanted any shopping. Mother called me to get ready and told me to just have a "lick and a promise" so that we did not miss the bus with the dolls house. We had just arranged for its transportation and started down York Road when we heard the plane screaming low, heard the frightening noise of bombs dropping and the siren wailing, all at the same time. The Heinkel 111 flew so low over the Rex buildings on its way out to sea that we could clearly see the insignia painted on its fuselage – a black cross outlined in white. The guns fired from HMS St Barbara (the pier), hit it, and it plunged into the sea. It was all so sudden, so noisy and so very frightening.

Mum shouted, "Our house! A bomb has hit our house!"

We rushed along the High Street to go into Lyon Street, but our way was barred by a warden until we told him that we lived at the far end of the street.

A sight of utter devastation awaited us. Earth had been flung everywhere, houses were damaged and when we reached our gate some people cheered – no-one had seen us leave and they had been searching for us. I could not push open our gate and had to climb over it. I ran round the back and found our house was all opened up like a doll's house. The flats had disappeared. Nothing remained but a huge pile of rubble with a large crater by its side. There was no sign of Mrs Grapes or any of the other inhabitants of the flats. It was heart-rending.

The remainder of our house had to be demolished as it was unsafe.

So now you can tell why a Victorian doll's house became so priceless to me. I would not be here to tell this story if it had not been given to me.

This photographer of me with my mother and father was taken during World War II.

Home at Last – Part I

We returned to the south of England in January 1945. My mother could not work anymore owing to ill health. She was advised not to stay in Yorkshire as it was too hilly for her to walk; her heart would not stand the exertion. She had spent three years as a war worker, first as a canteen worker in a large factory, then as a canteen manageress in another factory which had 800 workers. In addition to cooking lunch, the catering staff also had to supply mid-morning and afternoon trolley rounds. With only one main cook, four kitchen workers and one office worker, they all worked extremely hard.

In the school holidays I would accompany the trolley lady around the factory and found it fascinating. The factory workers had meals supplied at very low cost and the owners employed my mother and her staff to make the canteen non-profit making. However, although the prices were very low, she could not help but make a profit, even though a mug of tea was only one penny. First thing in the morning a number of workers wanted a slice of bread and dripping (also one penny). Coupled with a two-course lunch and two trolley rounds of tea and snacks per day meant they were all well catered for.

My father suggested we try something new that he had served in the army. It consisted of a jam sandwich dipped in batter and then deep-fried. Surprisingly, it tasted quite good! We would try almost anything during the war.

One of the canteen ladies was very lively and would often perform the can-can in the kitchen. 'Music while you work' was the background music played all the time over the Tannoy system; it was supposed to help production.

As our home in Lyon Street, Bognor Regis had been bombed in 1942, we stayed in Orchard Street, Chichester with my grandparents. My Granddad had died the previous November (1944), so I slept with Grandma in her feather bed. The house became overcrowded as various family members returned home.

My Auntie Ella and cousin Valerie returned from Canada where Uncle Tom had taught pilots in his capacity as a squadron leader. Their home in Coventry had been bombed, so they too were relying on Grandma until they found a place to live.

People had moved to Bognor Regis from Portsmouth and London during the war and stayed, so it was very difficult to find anywhere to live.

My cousin Brian and I cycled all around the neighbourhood, looking for an empty house and finally noticed a bungalow in Rose Green. We took a note of the number and cycled back to Chichester to tell my mother.

The next day we went to Bognor Regis town hall and, although it was a problem for Mum to climb the stairs right to the top floor she was determined to get a home again. She even carried a travel blanket in order to put her views across – with words to the effect that if we didn't get a house after being bombed out she was going to wrap me up in it and we would stay overnight on that top landing. At 14 years old I was very embarrassed by it all. Dr Michael Ayres listened to what she had to say and then called an emergency meeting. They found out who the landlord of the building was and requisitioned it for us.

Canadian troops had been billeted in the bungalow and it was in quite a state, but it was soon painted and gradually became a home. I had to do the majority of the housework, as Mum was still frail, but she was able to do the cooking.

The front garden had a trench dug out which we filled in. We wondered why we kept finding frogs on the front grass until a neighbour explained that there used to be a pond there.

I bought tomato plants and was very proud when I picked them. It was beginning to feel like a normal life again and just needed my Father home to make it complete.

One of the first things my father did when he came home was to ask me to cycle to Barnham market with him, where he bought some chicks. He had always wanted to keep poultry. Now we had a large back garden, he had his wish. He also grew tobacco plants and attempted to dry the leaves to make his own tobacco, although I never did ask him what it tasted like!

At last I was able to get a job. I worked at a chemists in Bognor High Street for about a year before deciding that I would prefer to work in an office. In September 1946, on my 16th birthday I started work at Wingards, the car accessory firm, which was situated in Kingsham Road, Chichester. I worked in the office as the Junior Ledger Clerk, checking through the files for new customers, bad debtors and 'dead' files. The filing system was in a mess. Most of our customers were garages, but some were filed under the name of the owner whereas others were filed under the name of the garage. In addition, they were filed by the county, rather than the town that they were situated in. Sorting it all out was quite time-consuming. I only have to hear a town name now and the county immediately comes to mind, nine times out of ten correctly!

The office consisted of one very large room where each department had its own line of workers – wages, invoices, sales etc. A number of ex-servicemen were there. I can still remember that there were two ex-Army, an ex-RAF man, an ex-sailor and I must not forget an ex-ATS woman. It must have been very tame for them after winning the war to have to 'win the peace'.

The factory was through the doors leading from the office. It also consisted of one huge room in which the only heating in winter came from a brazier situated at the centre. The canteen was in the far corner.

Later, my father worked in the factory, but as we started work at different times we had to make our separate ways there. I cycled in the summer but used the bus in the winter. My father worked there until he passed away in 1967.

I used to go dancing in Chichester as well as Bognor Regis. Sometimes I stayed overnight at my Auntie Win's in Velyn Avenue if I went to the Whyke Hall in Whyke Lane. Other times I caught the bus back after attending the Assembly Rooms dance on a Saturday night.

German and Italian prisoners of war were in huts around the Runcton/Mundham area, Germans one side of the road and Italians near the school. Often, on my way to work, I would see an Italian POW tending the allotment at the far end of the school playground. They also used the buses to go into Chichester. My feelings were mixed at the time, as I had lost my home and people I had known as a consequence of the war.

I cannot remember when the buses altered to having long seats upstairs, but I do remember that they were like that in the 1940s. The seats stretched from side to side with a gangway on the right.

In January 1948 I started work in Bognor Regis at the Gas and Electricity Company offices in Argyle Road as a Ledger Clarke. I thoroughly enjoyed the job as I had long rows of figures to add up at accounts balance time. We would have to search through to find one penny if we were out by that figure. We did not possess adding machines then and I still enjoy adding up figures without the aid of a calculator.

In the office we always attempted to get our invoices out before Bognor Regis Urban District Council sent out their annual rates demands. Whether it made any difference I am not certain, but it was friendly rivalry.

During the late 1940s the private gas and electricity companies were nationalised and the electricity workers in Bognor were transferred to Chichester. However, I was fortunate to stay in Bognor Regis working for the Gas Board.

Our bungalow at 112 Rose Green Road was on the left, just beyond the big farmhouse.

Rose Green Village Hall (bottom photo, on right) where I spent many happy nights at the local 'hops'.

Memories of Bognor Regis & Chichester in the 30s, 40s & 50s

The crossroads at Barrack Lane Aldwick as it used to look in the early 1900s. The Ship Inn can be seen in the distance.

Mum, Granddad Knight and Sylvia

Mum, Sylvia and 'Monty.

Three pictures from Wingard's Dance at 'Kimbells', Chichester 18th March 1950 which I attended with my parents.

Workers at Wingards, Kingsham Road Chichester c1950.

Wingard's outingin the 1950s. My mother is 2nd from left in the front row, my father standing behind her.

The Sweet Smell of the Past

I was fifteen when I started work at a chemists in the High Street - it was the time when assistants stood dutifully behind counters. Arranged along one wall were rows and rows of little square drawers with white china knobs, a letter on each drawer giving a clue to the initial letter of the products inside.

It was 1946 and although the war was over some products were still difficult to buy. Toilet soap was *very* difficult to come by so shaving sticks were used instead but were "under the counter". We were always told to ask the Manageress if we had any when a customer asked for one as she kept them for her acquaintances. I found it very embarrassing when she said "No!" when we knew that we had some.

We also sold perfume oil for six shillings a tiny phial. We had to gently pour it from a corked bottle and were told to always re-cork it straight away as a full bottle held £20 worth of perfume oil. I was only earning fifteen shilling (75p) a week, so it was like handling liquid gold.

One day I was serving a customer with a product which was stored under the counter and on putting my hand on the counter to straighten up, the bottle of perfume oil, which had been left uncorked, was knocked flying. The majority spilt on a stack of Izal toilet rolls, leaving them in an oily and overpowering smelly state!

No one owned up to leaving the bottle uncorked and I was not blamed as the bottle didn't smash, so would have remained intact if corked. I was very relieved as I would have had to work for twenty five weeks to pay for the spilt perfume.

The smell of perfume pervaded the shop for months but when customers remarked on the lovely smell I said 'please don't talk about it'. We managed to sell the toilet rolls and I told customers they were lucky to get perfume oil free of charge.

The Chemist's shop has now disappeared, but each time I pass that spot I fancy I can still smell that perfume…

Home at Last – Part II

I had been attending dances at the Pavilion for about three years. Later buses ran at midnight to take us to various parishes around the area, making it safe for those of us who lived outside Bognor Regis to attend these social events.

The Pavilion had the finest sprung dance floor on the South Coast. The large hall was used for many purposes, including roller skating and wrestling matches (I once saw 'Abdul the Turk' perform there after he had put down his prayer mat and prayed to Allah!). The Bognor Regis Horticultural Society had flower shows there, also the annual Memorial Service was held there. People could sit around in the restaurant; it was such a useful building.

All this ended in 1948 when the right-hand turret caught fire. I was on my way to the Co-op in Canada Grove to buy tobacco for my boss when I saw the fire. I rushed back to tell my fellow workers and we went to watch the firemen for a while. We could not believe it when it was later decided to demolish the Pavilion when it could so easily have been repaired.

The Rex Ballroom had been an alternative venue but now it became Bognor's only large venue for dancing. Famous bands performed there as they had in the past at the Pavilion. We danced to the melodic music of Syd Dean, Cyril Stapleton, Ivy Benson and her all-girl band, and the Ted Heath Orchestra, which was fronted by famous singers Dennis Lotis, Dickie Valentine and Lita Roza. I managed to get their autographs. It was a magical time for dance bands.

Living in Rose Green, as I did at that particular time, gave me the opportunity to take our dog 'Monty' out for walks and to really get to know my surroundings. In Hook Lane at that time there was a thriving brickyard where the 'Lion' bricks were made. My cousin Valerie and I used to stand at the gate to watch the men at work. I found out later that those particular bricks had a blue tinge and were more expensive than plain ones. Houses now occupy the site. In the 1940s there were only around 20 houses along there. My father and I used to collect mushrooms from the field behind Mant's farmhouse (now demolished – Rose Green school and social housing now occupy that area). Rose Green village hall was a meeting place for the young people of the area and we used to enjoy Saturday night 'hops' which were regularly held there. (The eerie call of the Owers lightship at night calling across the sea and sounding back across the fields is a memory that has stayed with me).

Jordan's store (Rose Green Stores) was at the corner of Rose Green Road and Carlton Avenue. The owners were very helpful to me when Dad was still in the army; they would let me use their phone to call the doctor when my mother had heart attacks.

Moore Marriott (the actor who played many roles in Will Hay films such as 'Oh Mr Porter!') and his family bought a shop in Rose Green Road. He became a family friend.

By this time my Auntie Ella, Uncle Tom and cousin Valerie had settled in Fernhurst Gardens. Auntie Ella was company for my mother and they attended whist drives in Rose Green Hall, where they made new friends.

Valerie and I attended confirmation classes given by the deaconess from St Richards Church in Gossamer Lane. The Rev Mosse was the vicar at that time and we were very honoured to be confirmed by the Bishop of Chichester, Bishop Bell.

Food and clothes were still on ration then so it was difficult to dress in all-white, as was the practice for confirmations. My outfit was black and white, the nearest I could get to being correctly dressed!

My first wedding was held at St Richards Church in 1950. The only way I managed to buy the material for my wedding dress was to exchange eggs from my father's chickens for clothing coupons.

My parents lived at Rose Green until 1st January 1955 when the ten year terms of requisition were almost up. By then, the bungalow was in a far better state than it had been when we moved in, the council having put in airbricks and new flooring; consequently the owner sold it at the earliest possible opportunity.

Although under the terms of war damage and demolition of buildings, original tenants should have been given their houses back, that did not happen in the case of my parents. When our home in Lyon Street was bombed in 1942, the landlord wrote in the rent book "until after the duration of war". Unfortunately he settled back into his own re-built home and sold the re-built house next door (our former house) instead of re-letting it to my parents.

On 1st January 1955 my mother and father moved into Corbishley Road. By that time I was a married woman and living in Lyon Street, next-door-but-one to where I had lived as a child. I also did letting there for a while, competing with almost every house in the street. I bought a bright blue and orange sign stating "Bed & Breakfast and Evening Meal". We started the season at Easter and vied for holiday-makers. Bognor Regis was such a busy place in those days. However, by the 1970s most people's holidays were spent abroad. Butlin's holiday camp opened in 1960, and caravan parks and industrial work in our area further eased the need for people to let rooms. Foreign students stayed with local families (no full board signs required) and then rising property prices encouraged the sub-division of family-sized houses into two, three or even four flats, reducing the number of places for letting and resulting in the disappearance of those many welcoming 'B&B' signs in the windows of Bognor's houses.

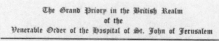

The Grand Priory in the British Realm
of the
Venerable Order of the Hospital of St. John of Jerusalem

THE ST. JOHN AMBULANCE BRIGADE
Bognor Regis Divisions

CORONATION FETE

Wednesday, August 12th, 1953, at 2.30 p.m.

Ruby Miller

Merchant Taylors Home Grounds
(By kind permission of the Matron and Governors)
High Street (nr. Bus Station) **Bognor Regis**

Lucky Souvenir Programme   *Threepence*

No. 806

ESPLANADE   THEATRE

BOGNOR REGIS - TELEPHONE: 1902

Entertainments Manager: C. E. POWELL, A.I.M.E.M.

SUNDAY, 18th AUGUST, 1957
at 8 p.m.

Edmund Hockridge

*Singing Star of T.V., Radio, Records, & Pajama Game,
Can-Can, Guys & Dolls, & Carousel*

IRVING KAYE
the South African Whistling Violinist

and His ORCHESTRA

INCLUDING

IDA WILLIS   **CICELY GORDON**
SONGS YOU WILL LOVE   AT THE PIANO

JIMMY BERRY
AT THE
Wonder Hammond Electronic Organ

Programme — Price Sixpence

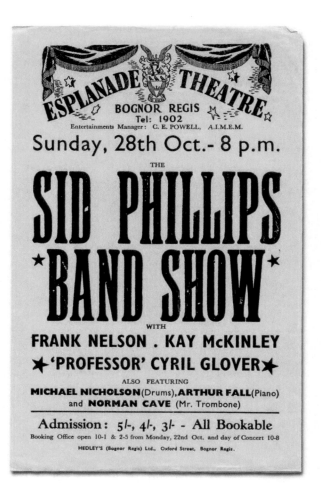

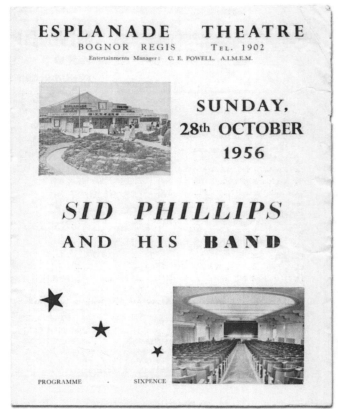

The Author, aged 18.

Bognor Regis Army Cadets c1947.
(left to right) Back row: Leon Morris, Leslie Ward, unknown, John Guppy.
Front row: Leslie Williams, unknown, Capt Williamson, Dennis Booker, Ken Olliver.

1949. Ken Olliver, who served in 14th/20th Kings Hussars and 3rd Carabiniers Prince of Wales Dragoon Guards.

My husband-to-be, Ken Olliver (on right!) outside Marine Park Café in Bognor Regis in the late 1940s. Where did all those lifelike ice-cream advertising figures go? Do you remember those long triangular 'Snofrutes' which we used to push up with our thumb? The cardboard cover would get all wet.

Proud mother and son John.

The staff at Bognor Regis Railway Station, May 20th 1949. (left to right) Bill Crook (porter), Tom Sutton (ticket collector), Dick Holcombe (passenger train shunter), Bill Taylor (ticket collector), Andy Bailey (passenger train shunter), Sid Bishop (Porter). Seated at the front is Fred Wickens, the stationmaster, who lived at 83 Longford Road, Bognor Regis (my schoolfriend's father – a very kind gentleman)

George Thomas Moore Marriott, the well-known film actor, who appeared alongside Will Hay in a series of popular comedy films of the 1940s, which included 'Oh Mr Porter!'. He moved to Rose Green and became a family friend until his death in 1949, aged 64.

Time & Tide

We walk together along the promenade
Talking of the changes, not for the better,
Of buildings demolished and sand disappearing
Under mounds of pebbles brought in
To stop the onslaught of the tide.

This is our seaside town
Where the fine sand slipped between our toes,
The tangy smell of the sea once pervaded our young bodies
Where we gazed half-afraid at Punch and Judy
Now we watch the children's faces as they sit transfixed.

Coach trip ladies sit cosily together,
Local ladies sit abjectly alone
Thinking of their partner whose sand of time has run out
They wonder why they retired to somewhere where they now sit alone.

I know that I am fortunate to walk side by side
With my partner, as they once did with theirs,
Talking of times and how they have changed,
But sadly we know that time and tide wait for no man
However high we build our defences.

Sylvia Olliver, 1994.

Postcards from Bygone Bognor

FOUNTAIN AND PRINCESS ELIZABETH BOATING POOL, BOGNOR REGIS. 2207.

Boating Pool and the sands.

THE SANDS, BOGNOR

WEST-END GARDENS, BOGNOR REGIS

West Parade

THE PROMENADE, BOGNOR REGIS. 115

SANDS WEST, BOGNOR REGIS

SANDS WEST, BOGNOR REGIS

EAST PARADE AND PIER, BOGNOR REGIS

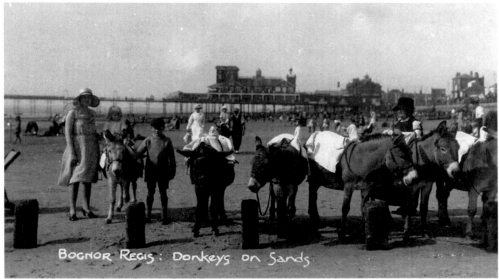

BOGNOR REGIS : Donkeys on Sands

BATHING HUTS W. PROMENADE 100

PIER, BOGNOR REGIS

Marine Park Gardens

The Steyne (above) and Hotham Park (below).

Chichester Cathedral Weather Cock, 1931

This sequence of pictures shows the re-positioning of the Chichester Cathedral weathervane in c1931. It received a number of pot-shots during World War 2 and has since been replaced.

Mind's Eye

When in my mind's eye snatched images from the past
Come into focus and then reveal
Like conjured-up snapshots which last in memory
But cannot put a positive seal

For parents who once with me shared
The times and maybe the memory of the place
By name or when and where,
Have entered the realm beyond the human race.

So as each picture comes back to review
I know that they exist somewhere
And at leisure I can imbue
My life with my own built in time share

Sylvia Olliver

York Road c1920.